THE A–Z OF MARZIPAN SWEETS

Commissioning Editor Rose Hewlett
Words by Sophie Berry
Illustrations and Design by Zoë Horn Haywood

ALMONDS

Marzipan is made from a mixture of sugar or honey, and almond meal. Almond meal is very finely ground almonds, and gives many marzipan sweets their distinctive flavour. Try this simple and straightforward recipe for classic, uncooked marzipan.

Classic Uncooked Marzipan

Ingredients
- ½ cup confectioners' sugar
- ½ cup granulated sugar
- 2 cups ground almonds
- 2 egg whites
- ¼ tsp flavouring (optional)
- ¼ tsp colouring (optional)

Method
1. In a large bowl, sift together the sugar, then add the almonds and mix well.

2. Beat the egg whites until they are frothy, and fold them into the sugar and almond mixture.

3. Add the extract and colouring, and knead well to create a stiff paste. Add a little extra sugar if the mixture is too wet.

4. Allow the mixture to stand for a few hours, then shape into sweets by hand. You can also roll the marzipan out flat on a cool work surface powdered with icing sugar and use cutters to shape.

5. Use the marzipan as soon as possible as it won't store for longer than 24 hours.

BOILED MARZIPAN

Marzipan can be made in a number of ways. The main difference in recipes is whether the marzipan mixture is cooked, or uncooked. This simple recipe for simple, boiled marzipan is a great place to start if you'd like to try a cooked version of the sweet treat.

Simple Boiled Marzipan

Ingredients
1 lb granulated sugar
½ cup water
2 cups ground almonds
1 tbsp glucose
1 tsp almond flavouring
½ cup icing sugar

Method
1. In a large saucepan over a low heat, dissolve the sugar and water and add the glucose.

2. Boil the mixture, stirring constantly, until the mixture reaches 245°F, or until the mixture forms a firm ball when tested in cold water.

3. Remove the pan from the heat, and add the almonds and almond flavouring.

4. Carefully turn the mixture out onto a marble slab, or other heat safe work surface.

5. When the mixture is cool enough to handle, knead until smooth. Dust your hands and work surface with the icing sugar to prevent the marzipan becoming sticky.

6. Roll small pieces of marzipan into balls, and dust with a little icing sugar.

7. Store somewhere cool.

CUPS

Lots of recipes in this book will use 'cups' as a measurement. A small coffee cup is perfect for this, and as long as you use the same cup for all measurements, any cup will do.

Below is a handy conversion table

1 cup	8 fluid ounces	½ pint	237 ml
2 cups	16 fluid ounces	1 pint	474 ml
4 cups	32 fluid ounces	1 quart	946 ml
2 pints	32 fluid ounces	1 quart	0.946 l
4 quarts	128 fluid ounces	1 gallon	3.784 l

DROP TEST

The 'drop test' is when you drop a little marzipan mixture into cold water to test the temperature of the boiling sugar mixture. If you are using a recipe which requires cooking, it is a quick and easy way to see if your marzipan mixture is ready to take off the heat without using a thermometer.

This handy table shows what to look out for at all stages when you are cooking with sugar.
The temperature that you are required to heat your mixture to will vary from recipe to recipe, so make sure you check carefully before you start making your marzipan.

Stage	Temperature	Uses
Thread - Forms a thin liquid thread	110°C to 112 °C (230 to 234 °F)	Sugar Syrups
Soft ball - Forms a soft flexible ball that can be flattened.	112°C to 116 °C (234 to 241 °F)	Fudge, pralines, fondant and butter creams
Firm ball - Forms a firm ball that will hold its shape but is still malleable	118°C to 120 °C (244 to 248 °F)	Caramel Candies
Hard ball - Forms thick threads from spoon and creates a hard ball that will hold its shape	121 to 130 °C (250 to 266 °F)	Nougat, marshmallows, gummies, and divinity
Soft crack - Forms firm flexible threads	132°C to 143 °C (270 to 289 °F)	salt water taffy
Hard crack - Forms hard brittle threads that snap easily	146°C to 154 °C (295 to 309 °F)	toffee, brittles, hard candy, and lollipops
Clear liquid - Liquid will begin to change colour. Colour ranges from golden brown to amber	160 °C (320 °F)	caramelised sugar, caramel
Brown liquid - Liquid will begin to change colour. Colour ranges from golden brown to amber	170 °C (338 °F)	caramelised sugar, caramel

EGGS

Eggs are a key ingredient in many marzipan recipes. Eggs will give your marzipan a rich, pliable texture. Some recipes will call for you to use egg whites only, and others state egg yolks only. This recipe is slightly unusual in that you can use either egg whites or yolks. Both will give similar results, and you can try making it both ways to see which version you prefer.

Rich Marzipan

Ingredients
1 lb sugar
3 cups ground almonds
2 egg whites, or 2 egg yolks
½ cup water
1 tbsp glucose
1 lb shop-bought fondant

Method
1. In a heavy-bottomed saucepan dissolve the sugar in the water, then add the glucose and heat the mixture until the thermometer reads 240°F, or until the mixture forms a soft ball when tested in cold water.

2. Remove the pan from the heat, and stir in the almonds.

3. The paste should be fairly stiff at this point.

4. When the mixture has cooled slightly, add the beaten egg whites, or beaten egg yolks and heat gently until the mixture won't adhere to the sides of the pan.

5. Remove the pan from the heat and carefully pour the mixture onto a marble slab, or other heat safe work surface.

6. When the mixture is cool enough to handle, knead until smooth.

7. Lay the marzipan out onto baking parchment, and leave it to stand somewhere cool for 24 hours before using.

FRUIT

Fruit flavours work well with marzipan, and you can even get creative and shape your marzipan sweets into miniature pieces of fruit. These make perfect presents, and can also be used to decorate cakes or desserts.

Lots of fruits work well in marzipan sweets, but chopped dried fruits are easiest to work into the marzipan mixture. This recipe for bite-sized cherry marzipan sweets is straightforward, simple and requires no cooking. Feel free to substitute cherries for a different fruit if you prefer.

Cherry Marzipan

Ingredients
½ cup confectioners' sugar
½ cup granulated sugar
2 cups ground almonds
1 cup chopped glace cherries
2 egg whites
¼ tsp cherry flavouring
¼ tsp red colouring

Method
1. In a large bowl, sift together the sugar, then add the almonds and mix well.

2. Beat the egg whites until they are frothy, and fold them into the sugar and almond mixture.

3. Add the extract and colouring, and knead well to create a stiff paste. Add a little extra sugar if the mixture is too wet.

4. Sprinkle the chopped cherries onto your work surface, and roll the mixture over them. Blend the cherries into the marzipan mixture by kneading well.

5. Allow the mixture to stand for a few hours, then shape into bite-sized balls by hand.

6. Use the marzipan as soon as possible as it won't store for longer than 24 hours.

GOLDEN MARZIPAN

This recipe for golden marzipan uses an egg, as well as an extra egg yolk for a lovely rich finish. It's a really easy recipe to master, and doesn't involve any cooking at all. It will need to stand for 24 hours before being ready to use though, so make sure you plan ahead and get your golden marzipan prepared the day before.

Golden Marzipan

Ingredients
1 cup confectioners' sugar
2 cups ground almonds
1 egg
1 egg yolk
¼ tsp salt
¼ tsp almond extract
1 tbsp icing sugar, to dust

Method
1. In a large bowl, mix all the ingredients together with a wooden spoon except the icing sugar.

2. Keep mixing until your ingredients are well combined and form a firm ball of dough.

3. Cover the bowl with a damp towel, and allow the mixture to stand for 24 hours before shaping.

4. Roll small pieces of marzipan into balls, and dust with a little icing sugar.

5. Store somewhere cool.

HONEY

Honey was a key ingredient in the earliest versions of marzipan which started to appear during the Middle Ages. Honey was used in place of sugar, and acted as a bonding agent as well as adding a sweetness to the distinctive flavour of the nuts used.

This recipe for honey pistachio marzipan sweets uses sugar as well as honey, for a more subtle honey flavour. Pistachios have long been used to make marzipan, and vibrantly green pistachio marzipan is a traditional delicacy in parts of Mexico.

Honey Pistachio Marzipan

Ingredients
2 cups shelled unsalted pistachios
1 tbsp caster sugar
2 tbsp clear runny honey
1 tbsp lemon juice
1 tbsp icing sugar, to dust

Method
1. Put the pistachio nuts and caster sugar into a food processor and pulse until the mixture resembles coarse breadcrumbs. Do not over-process, otherwise the nuts may release their oils and become greasy. Drizzle in the honey and lemon juice and blend until the mixture starts to clump together.

2. Turn the marzipan onto a smooth work surface dusted with icing sugar and knead lightly until your mixture is soft and smooth.

3. Roll your marzipan out flat to a thickness of about ¼" and cut into small squares.

4. Store somewhere cool.

ICING

One of the main uses of marzipan is as a topping for cakes. Marzipan lends itself well to heavy, rich fruit cakes in particular, as smoothing a layer onto the cake creates a wonderfully smooth surface for you to start decorating. Marzipan is often used alongside white royal icing, which is similar in texture to marzipan. You can buy ready-to-roll icing if you wish to add a layer of this on top of your marzipan.

Icing a cake with marzipan is a fairly straightforward task. Read our step-by-step guide, and you'll be ready to roll!

Before you start, you will need to prepare a little apricot jam to use to bond the marzipan to your cake. Heating the jam, and passing it through a sieve will make brushing it onto your cake much easier. Use a pastry brush to spread a little jam over the cake you are covering with marzipan.

A good marzipan recipe you can use for this is the Classic Uncooked Marzipan recipe at the start of this book.

1. On a smooth work surface, knead your marzipan to make it pliable and soft. A sprinkling of icing sugar on your work surface and hands will stop it becoming sticky.

2. Take a rolling pin, sprinkle it with a little icing sugar, and start gently pressing down onto your ball of marzipan.

3. Continue carefully rolling and rotating your marzipan by 90° until it is about 3mm thick. Now, pick up the marzipan by rolling it over your rolling pin and lifting it off your work surface.

4. Carefully lay the marzipan onto your apricot jam-covered cake. Smooth over with icing sugar-dusted hands, and trim the excess at the base of the cake.

If you wish to add a layer of icing on top of the marzipan, simply repeat this process with the icing, and lay it on top, not forgetting the apricot jam.

20

JAM

Jam is a useful addition to your store cupboard if you are planning to use marzipan as a cake covering. Apricot jam works best, as it is subtly coloured and won't stain your marzipan. Heat the jam up slightly to make it easier to spread, and pass it through a sieve to remove any lumpy fruit pieces. Gently brush the warmed jam onto your cake's surface, and smooth over your marzipan immediately.

Jam will also be very useful if you are planning to make and shape marzipan into sweets. It can be used in small amounts as an adhesive to stick small pieces together, when making marzipan flowers or fruit for example. You can also use it to glaze your marzipan, which will give your sweets a slight sheen as well as a subtle pop of colour.

KNEADING

Kneading is an important part of the preparation method when making marzipan. It allows your ingredients to be thoroughly combined, and will give your finished product a lovely, smooth consistency.

If you are using a cooked marzipan recipe, make sure it is cool enough to handle before you start kneading. You will need a good work surface to knead your marzipan on. A kitchen worktop is fine, or you could use a glass or marble chopping board.

A sprinkling of icing sugar on your work surface and your hands will also stop your marzipan from becoming too sticky while you work it. Using the heel of your hand, push the ball of marzipan away from you, folding the edges onto themselves and repeating the kneading motion.

If you're using a board to work your marzipan on, you can store the board in the fridge before use. The cool surface will also stop your marzipan from becoming too sticky as you knead.

LEMON MARZIPAN

Lemon marzipan, which is also called Manzapades, is a traditional recipe from the Jewish community in Greece and has been made there for hundreds of years. This recipe is slightly challenging in that it takes a couple of days to prepare, but the distinctive, zingy taste of lemon works brilliantly with the classic flavour of almonds in this recipe for marzipan. We think it is well worth the extra time it takes to make this original and unusual confectionery.

Lemon Marzipan or Manzapades

Ingredients
The dried lemon peels of 12 lemons
1 cup blanched almonds, finely ground
2 cups granulated sugar
1 cup icing sugar

Method
1. Put the lemon peels in a bowl, and cover them with water. Leave them to soak for two days, changing the water every 3-4 hours.

2. On the third day, rinse the peels and put them into a large saucepan with water to cover. Place over low heat and simmer for 45 to 60 minutes, until peels are very soft.

3. Remove the pan from the heat and pulse the peel in a food processor. You should have about one cup of pulp.

4. Return the pulp to the large saucepan and add the ground almonds and 2 cups of granulated sugar. Mix well and place over low heat. Stir often with a wooden spoon. Cook until the mixture thickens and starts peeling away from the pan sides.

5. Remove the pan from the heat and pour onto a marble slab or other smooth work surface.

6. When the mixture has cooled slightly, spread the powdered sugar onto a separate plate. Knead the mixture a little and then pinch off pieces the size of hazelnuts. Roll them into balls and then roll in the powdered sugar.

7. Allow the marzipan to rest for 24 hours before serving.

MOLDING

The beauty of marzipan is that once you have made a batch, you can shape and mould it into pretty much anything you like. It has a wonderfully pliable texture, and is very easy to work with. You can mold marzipan into flowers or miniature pieces of fruit for beautiful finishing touches to a cake on a special occasion. Carefully wrapped marzipan sweets also make for a thoughtful and unusual gift. A light dusting of icing sugar on your hands and work surface should stop things getting too sticky.

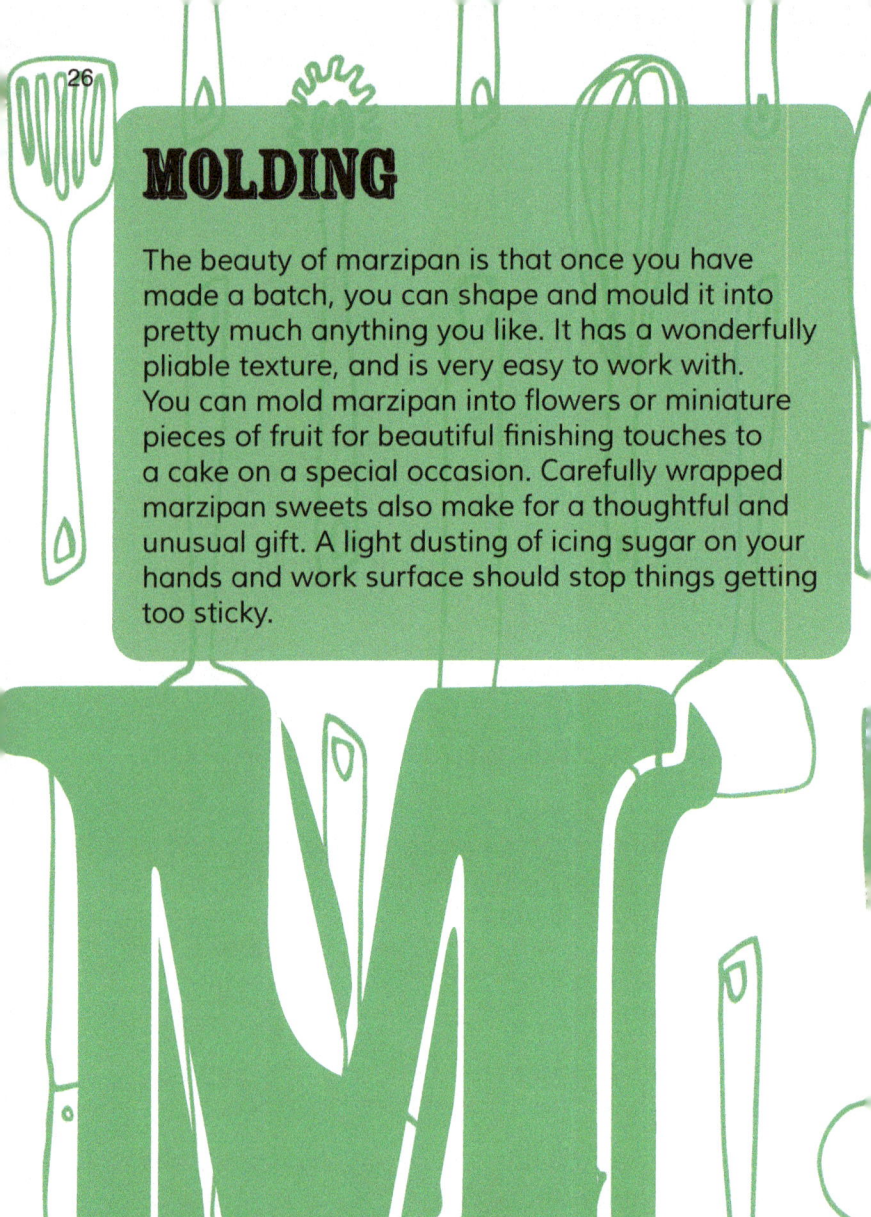

Here are some great tips and tricks for molding your marzipan sweets.

- Rolling your sweets over a zest grater will give a wonderful texture, or you could try running a fork or serrated knife over the surface of your sweets.

- A cocktail stick is a handy tool, and can be used to create texture, or add detail to the surface of your sweets.

- Small cookie cutters are a quick and easy way to shape your marzipan sweets. Roll your marzipan to about ¼" thick first.

- Kneading food colouring through your marzipan is an easy way of getting a smooth, even colour to your sweets. However, painting colouring on with a fine brush allows you to achieve a much more intricate finish.

- Dusting your sweets with ground spices is an easy way to add colour as well as flavour to your marzipan. Cinnamon and nutmeg work well with marzipan and gently rolling your sweets over a mixture of spices and icing sugar creates a wonderful mottled effect.

- Cloves are useful, and can be used to mimic stalks for your marzipan fruit.

- Using real leaves, cloves or small herbs to adorn your marzipan sweets can be really effective. Just remember to remove them before you enjoy them!

- Liquorice is useful when decorating your marzipan sweets as it can be used to adorn fruit and vegetable-shaped marzipan, as stalks for example.

NUTS

The instantly recognisable flavour of almonds is the basis of most marzipan sweets. However, you can experiment with using any kind of nut you like in your marzipan. Marzipan has been made in different forms all around the world for hundreds of years, and lots of countries have their own twist on the recipe. Cashew nuts are used in India to make a sweet like marzipan called Kaju Barfi. Try this great recipe for cashew marzipan, inspired by the traditional recipe for Kaju Barfi.

Kaju Barfi

Ingredients
3 cups sugar
1 cup water
5 cups ground cashew nuts
¼ tsp orange flavouring
¼ tsp colouring

Method
1. In a large saucepan, dissolve the sugar and water and add the cashews.

2. Heat the mixture gently, stirring constantly, until the mass will not adhere to the pan.

3. Remove the pan from the heat and carefully pour the mixture onto a marble slab, or other heat safe work surface.

4. When the mixture is cool enough to handle, knead until smooth, adding the colouring and flavouring while the mixture is still warm.

5. Roll out to about ½" thickness.

6. Cut into bite-sized squares. Store somewhere cool.

ORIGINS

It is very difficult to trace the origins of marzipan. Versions of the nut-based confectionery appear all over the world, and the sweet treat has been crafted by generations of cooks. Some say that the original recipe for marzipan originated in China, and came to be popular in Europe by travelling through the Medieval Muslim state, Al- Adalus. Al-Adalus was comprised of parts of what are now Spain, France, Portugal and Gibraltar.

However, some people believe that marzipan originates from Persia, and made it to Europe via Turkey. Konigsberg in Prussia is also a renowned for its marzipan manufacturing, and Konigsberg marzipan refers to a specific type of marzipan which has a burnt top, and added candied fruit. Sicily is another place where marzipan has been made for hundreds of years, and panis martius, or 'March bread' as it is called there, is a traditional Sicilian confectionery.

PARZIPAN

Parzipan is a version of marzipan which can be made with apricot kernels or peach kernels. This sweet treat originated in Germany and is also referred to as Persipan. If you'd like to use peach or apricot kernels instead of almonds, you will need to grind them up into a very fine grain.

Persipan consists of 40% ground kernels and 60% sugar. The kernels have a stronger flavour than almonds which some might find slightly bitter, but many people actually prefer the taste to classic almond-based marzipan. Finding a use for peach or apricot kernels can be difficult meaning they often go to waste. This makes persipan much cheaper to produce than marzipan.

 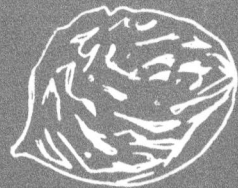 

LIQUEUR

Adding a dash of liqueur to your marzipan is a great way to add an extra kick of flavour, as well as making it a truly indulgent treat. You can use any liqueur you wish, although Amaretto works brilliantly. Made from almonds, Amaretto is the perfect addition to marzipan. Other nut liqueurs you could use include Frangelico (hazelnuts and herbs), or Dumante (pistachios).

Double Almond Marzipan

Ingredients
3 cups sugar
5 cups ground almonds
1 cup water
1 tbsp Amaretto
½ cup icing sugar

Method
1. In a heavy-bottomed saucepan dissolve the sugar and water over a low heat.

2. Add the almonds, and stir until the mixture won't adhere to the sides of the pan.

3. Carefully turn the mixture out onto a marble slab or other heatsafe work surface.

4. When the mixture is cool enough to handle, knead well.

5. Make a well in the middle of your ball of kneaded mixture, and gradually pour in the Amaretto, kneading the marzipan to blend.

6. If the marzipan mixture is too wet, add a little icing sugar as you knead. If the mixture is too dry, add a drop more Amaretto.

7. Take small pieces of marzipan and roll into bite-sized balls.

8. Dust the balls with icing sugar, and store somewhere cool.

RAISINS

Dried fruits work brilliantly in marzipan, and can really lift the flavour of your marzipan, complementing the distinctive almond taste. Raisins are the perfect addition as they are small, and will blend well with your mixture. You can even chop your raisins to make them finer, and give your marzipan a smoother texture.

Raisin Marzipan

Ingredients
4 tbsp raisins
1 egg white
¾ cup ground almonds
cup confectioners' sugar
½ tsp rose extract
¼ tsp almond extract
tsp red food colouring
½ cup icing sugar, for dusting

Method
1. In a large bowl, beat the egg white until it is stiff, and then sift in the confectioners' sugar.

2. Add the almonds, raisins, extracts and colouring to the egg white and sugar and mix well until the mixture takes on a dough-like consistency.

3. Carefully turn the mixture out onto a smooth work surface, dusted with icing sugar.

4. Dust a rolling pin with a little icing sugar, and roll the mixture out to about ¼" thick.

5. Use small cookie cutters to shape your marzipan.

STUFFED FRUITS

Stuffing fruits with marzipan is a great way to make a sweets with a hint of the distinctive flavour, without it being too overpowering. Added to this, the almond flavour works brilliantly with lots of fruits, especially sticky fruits like prunes, dates and cherries.

Prunes are the perfect size to stuff with marzipan. They are just small enough to be bite sized, but won't be too fiddly to prepare. Here's a great recipe for stuffed prunes for you to try. The Simple Uncooked Marzipan recipe at the start of this book is perfect for using to stuff fruits with, and is really straightforward to make.

Stuffed Prunes

Ingredients
1 cup prunes
2 oz Cooked Marzipan
2 cups sugar
½ cup water
¼ tsp cream of tartar
½ cup chopped coconut or chopped pistachio nuts

Method
1. Stone the prunes, and carefully fill the cavity with marzipan.

2. In a heavy-bottomed saucepan, dissolve the sugar in the water, add the cream of tartar and heat the mixture until it reaches 290°F, or the mixture forms firm, flexible strands when tested in cold water.

3. Leave the mixture to cool slightly, then carefully dip each prune into the syrup.

4. Roll the prunes in the coconut or pistachio, and leave to dry on a plate somewhere cool.

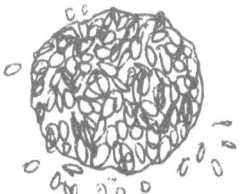

THERMOMETER

A thermometer is the best way to test the temperature of your marzipan mixture as it cooks, if you are using a recipe which requires cooking. Although you can test the mixture by dropping a little into cold water, a thermometer is far more accurate especially as the temperature of cooking sugar can soar extremely quickly.

Make sure you 'break in' a new thermometer. Put it into a pan of cold water, bring the pan to the boil, and leave it there until the water has cooled. After using your thermometer to test the temperature, plunge it into warm water and wipe it straight away.

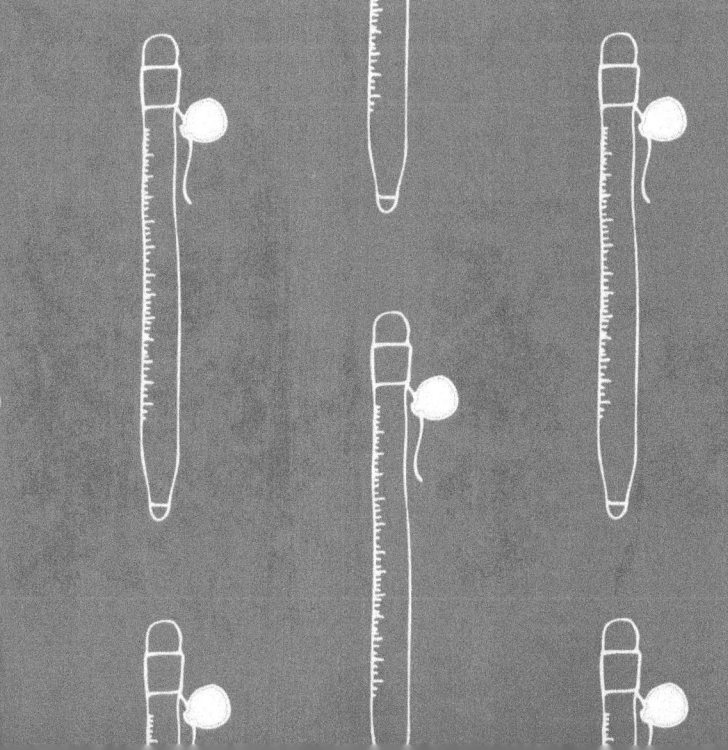

UTENSILS

Good utensils are essential when you are making marzipan, and a good wooden spoon is key. Some marzipan recipes will require heating the mixture to a high temperature, and a wooden spoon is best for stirring as plastic utensils won't withstand the high temperature of the boiling sugar.

You will also need a large, heavy bottomed saucepan, a large mixing bowl, and an electric hand whisk if you are using beaten egg whites in your marzipan. A sharp knife for chopping nuts and dried fruit finely is also useful, although a food processor can be used for this, too.

You will also need to source some utensils to mold and shape your marzipan sweets. Small cookie cutters, and other utensils which you can use to texture and shape your sweets will be really useful.

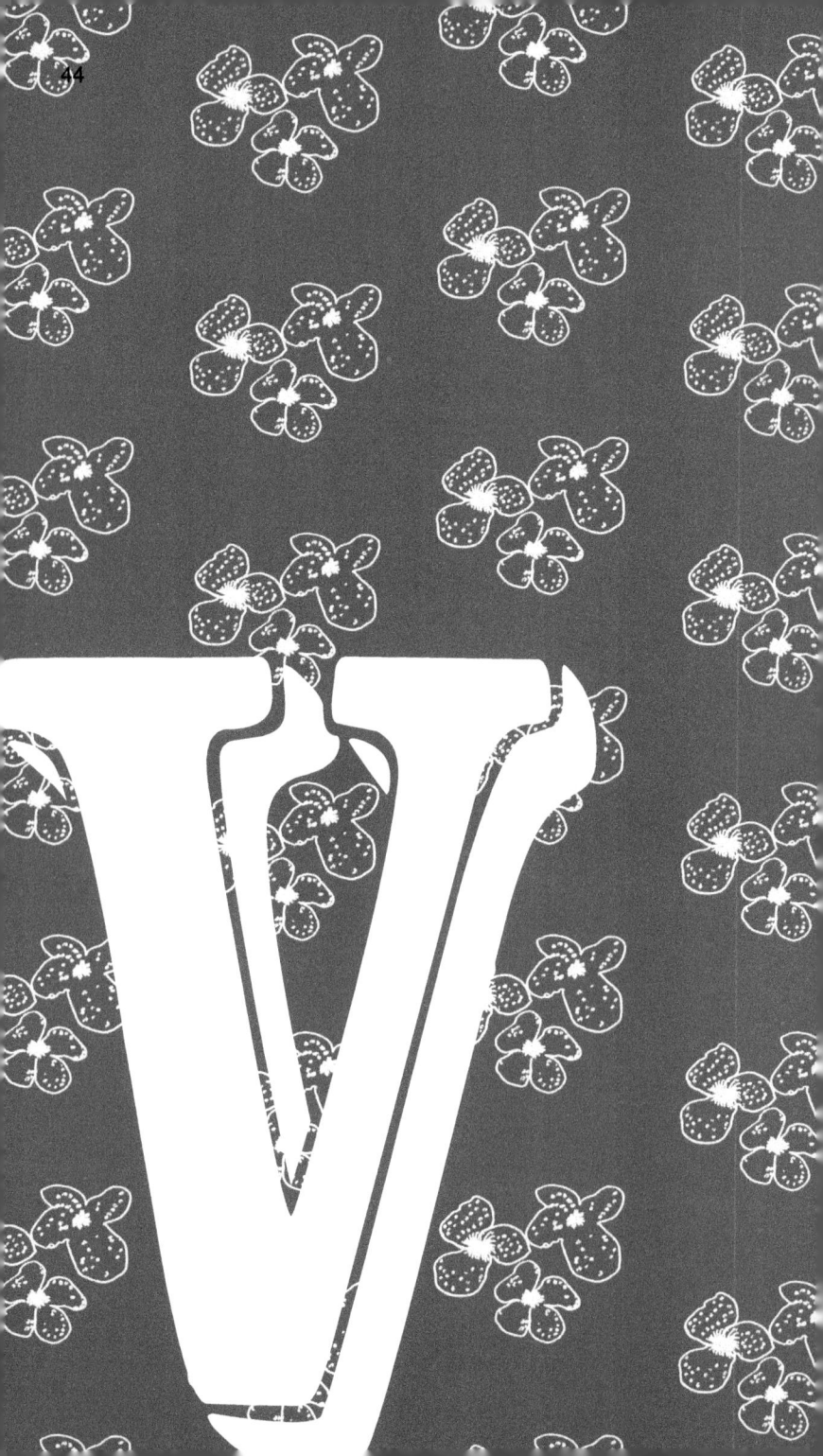

VIOLET BALLS

This unusual recipe uses candied violets, giving your marzipan a beautiful lilac hue. These pretty little balls make perfect decorations for cakes, or can be served on their own as a dainty sweet treat.

<u>Violet Balls</u>

<u>Ingredients</u>
3 egg whites
4 oz Cooked Marzipan
1 tsp vanilla extract
½ cup crushed, candied violets
½ cup icing sugar

<u>Method</u>
1. In a large bowl, beat two of the egg whites to a stiff froth, and add the marzipan, vanilla extract, and sprinkle the icing sugar in gradually.

2. You are aiming for a stiff paste, so keep carefully adding the icing sugar until you have the right consistency.

3. Use the rest of the icing sugar to lightly dust a smooth work surface and your hands, and knead the marzipan.

4. Beat the remaining egg white into a stiff froth, and set aside for a moment.

5. Form small balls out of your mixture, and dip them into the beaten egg white.

6. Roll the balls in crushed candied violets, and leave them to dry on a plate somewhere cool.

W

WALNUTS

Using walnuts to add crunch and extra flavour to your marzipan sweets works very well. They also add colour and decoration to the confectionery. You can use any flavours and all different kinds of nuts. Try this recipe for coffee and walnut marzipan bites for the perfect coffee break treat.

Coffee and Walnut Marzipan Bites

Ingredients
4 oz Cooked Marzipan
1 shot of espresso/ ½ cup strong coffee
1 cup walnut meats

Method
1. Dust a smooth work surface with icing sugar, and start kneading your cooked marzipan.

2. While it is still a ball, make a well in the marzipan and carefully pour in the coffee. You will have to do this gradually, or the coffee will not be absorbed by the marzipan.

3. Carefully knead the marzipan, blending the coffee into the mixture.

4. Form small balls from your coffee marzipan, and press two walnut halves onto the sides.

5. Serve straightaway.

XMAS

Christmas is the perfect time to show off your marzipan-making skills. As well as being used as a traditional Christmas cake topping, you can mold marzipan and use it to decorate the top of your iced cake, too. Marzipan sweets also make wonderful gifts, and with a few pots of colouring and flavouring can be made into just about anything you like.

Try this quirky recipe for Marzipan Christmas Puddings

Marzipan Christmas Puddings

Ingredients
½ cup confectioners' sugar
½ cup granulated sugar
2 cups ground almonds
2 egg whites
1 tsp grated nutmeg
2 tbsp dried cranberries, finely chopped.

Method
1. In a large bowl, sift together the sugar, then add the almonds and mix well.

2. Beat the egg whites until they are frothy, and fold them into the sugar and almond mixture.

3. Add the cranberries, and knead well to create a stiff paste. Add a little extra sugar if the mixture is too wet.

4. Allow the mixture to stand for a few hours, then shape small pieces of the marzipan into balls.

5. Sprinkle the grated nutmeg onto a plate, and carefully roll the balls in it to create a mottled, speckled finish.

6. Use the marzipan as soon as possible as it won't store for longer than 24 hours.

YOUNGSTERS

Making marzipan with children is great fun, and molding and shaping marzipan is a brilliant activity to do with children. The beauty of marzipan is that many of the recipes require no cooking. This is great if you are cooking with children, as you don't have to worry about accidents with hot sugar.

Children can shape and mould marzipan into an array of different designs, and use their imaginations to create some wonderful sweets. Marzipan is a pliable yet also quite durable dough, and will withstand lots of kneading and shaping. A little food colouring can be blended into the marzipan, so you can work with an array of different coloured dough, and really get creative.

ZEST

Adding the zest and juice of citrus fruits is a great way to add flavour to your marzipan, as well as a bright pop of colour. This recipe for zesty marzipan uses the zest and juice of an orange, but any citrus fruit will work well in this recipe. Experiment with a few versions and see which you prefer.

<u>Orange Marzipan</u>

<u>Ingredients</u>
2 cups caster sugar
2 cups icing sugar, plus extra for dusting
3 cups ground almonds
Grated zest and juice 1 orange
1 egg
1 egg yolk

<u>Method</u>
1. In a large bowl, sift the sugar and almonds together, then stir in the orange zest.

2. Beat together the egg and egg yolk and add to the sugar mixture, stirring well.

3. Carefully turn the mixture out onto a smooth work surface and knead well.

4. Add a little orange juice if the mix is too dry, or icing sugar if too wet.

5. Shape small amounts of marzipan into oranges, rolling them over a zest grater to give a textured finish. You can even add a clove as a stalk to make them look even more realistic.

6. Store somewhere cool.

TOP TEN TIPS

1. Buy a thermometer – It will make your marzipan-making a lot simpler, and much more accurate

2. Make sure you 'break in' a new thermometer. Put the thermometer into a pan of cold water, bring the pan to the boil, and leave it there until the water has cooled.

3. After using your thermometer to test the temperature, plunge it into warm water and wipe it straight away.

4. Have all your ingredients measured and ready before you begin. Marzipan making is very precise, and having everything ready will ensure nothing is overcooked.

5. Follow the recipe exactly. Until you have a lot of marzipan-making experience, it is best to follow recipes exactly. When you become more confident, you can experiment with your own variations.

AND TRICKS

6. Once you have poured the mixture out of the pan, immediately fill it with hot water and return it to the heat for a few minutes. This will stop your mixture setting onto the pan and will make it a lot easier to clean.

7. Take your marzipan out of the fridge at least five minutes before using it to ensure it won't be too hard to work with.

8. Dust your hands and your work surface with icing sugar when working with marzipan. This will stop your marzipan becoming too sticky.

9. Marzipan does not stay fresh for very long, so make sure you make it as near to when you need to use it as possible.

10. Marzipan is best stored in an airtight container in the fridge.

Copyright © 2013 Two Magpies Publishing
An imprint of Read Publishing Ltd
Home Farm, 44 Evesham Road, Cookhill, Alcester,
Warwickshire, B49 5LJ

Commissioning Editor Rose Hewlett
Words by Sophie Berry
Design and Illustrations by Zoë Horn Haywood

This book is copyright and may not be reproduced or copied in any way without the express permission of the publisher in writing.

British Library Cataloguing-in-Publication Data A catalogue record for this book is available from the British Library.

www.ingramcontent.com/pod-product-compliance
Lightning Source LLC
Chambersburg PA
CBHW070209100426
42743CB00013B/3119